The
Memory Verse
BIBLE
Storybook

The
Memory Verse
BIBLE
Storybook

by
K. Christie Bowler
Illustrated by Patricia Jaster

HOLMAN
BIBLE PUBLISHERS

Nashville, Tennessee

The Memory Verse Bible Storybook

© Copyright 2001 Lightwave Publishing Inc. All Rights Reserved

Published in 2001 by Holman Bible Publishers, Nashville, Tennessee

ISBN 0-8054-9417-0
Dewey Decimal Classification: 220.076
Subject Heading: Bible—Memorizing

For Lightwave
Concept and Direction: *Rick Osborne*
Art Director and Desktop: *Terry Van Roon*

The Singing Bible © Copyright 1993 Lightwave Publishing Inc.
Words and music Elaine Osborne pp. 132–135, Suzanne Mitchell
pp. 144–145, Robert Chapple p. 154

Scripture taken from the HOLMAN CHRISTIAN STANDARD BIBLE
© Copyright 1999, 2000 Holman Bible Publishers

Library of Congress Cataloging-in-Publication Data

Bowler, K. Christie, 1958–
    The memory verse Bible / by K. Christie Bowler ; illustrations by
Patricia Jaster.
        p. cm.
    ISBN 0-8054-9417-0
    1. Bible—Memorizing. 2. Bible—Study and teaching (Early child-
hood) I. Jaster, Patricia, 1938– ill. II. Title.

BS617.7 B69 2001
220'.076—dc21

00-054066

Printed in Korea
1 2 3 4 5 05 04 03 02 01
SW

Table of Contents

How To Use This Book 7

Memory Verses

God Made Every-
    thing 10
God Made You 12
Don't Eat from the
    Tree! 14
Noah and the Ark 16
Nothing Is Too Hard
    for God 18
Abraham Believed 20
A Great Nation 22
Face to Face.................... 24
Humble Moses 26
Compassionate God 28
The Ten Command-
    ments 30
The Blessing 32
Be Strong and
    Courageous.............. 34

I'll Go Where You
    Go 36
God Looks Inside 38
A Man After God's
    Heart 40
Shepherd's Psalm 42
Get Wisdom 44
Choose Life 46
God Has Plans 48
Good Daniel 50
Esther's Days 52
You'll Have a Son 54
Jesus Is Born 56
Jesus Grows Up 58
This Is My Son 60
Fishers of Men 62
Twelve Disciples 64
Jesus' Work 66
The Blesseds 68
Love Your Enemies 70
The Lord's Prayer 72

Seek the Kingdom 74
Lost or Found? 76
Do to Others 78
Jesus Is God 80
Small Faith 82
Children, Come! 84
The Greatest Com-
    mandments 86
Jesus Is the Way 88
The Holy Spirit 90
Jesus' Friends 92
Jesus Is Crucified 94
Jesus Is Risen 96
God Loved the
    World 98
Open the Door 100
Speak It Out 102
The Great
    Commission 104
Go Forward 106
Love 108
Fruit of the Spirit 110
Be Kind 112
Obey Your Parents 114
Be Happy 116
God's Word 118
Meet Together 120
Resist the Devil 122
God Forgives 124
God Is Love 126
The Father's House 128
No More Tears 130

Activities/Songs

Books of the Bible 132
Don't Eat from the
    Tree 136
Abraham Believed 137
The Ten Command-
    ments 138
God Looks Inside 140
Choose Life 141
You'll Have a Son 142
Twelve Disciples 144
Love Your Enemies 146
The Greatest Com-
    mandments 148
God Loved the
    World 150
The Great Commis-
    sion 151
Love 152
Fruit of the Spirit 154
God's Word 155
Miscellaneous Memor-
    izing Tips 156

How to Use this Book

The Memory Verse Bible Storybook will help your children memorize key verses from the Bible while giving them an introduction to God's Word. Key Scripture verses are tied into a summary of a Bible story, showing how the verse fits into the big picture of the Bible.

Why These Verses?

The verses and passages in this storybook have been carefully chosen to accomplish several purposes. When your children have memorized the verses they will:

- understand God's plan from Creation through the fall to Jesus' ministry, death, and resurrection, and on to heaven,
- have a basic understanding of how God loves and cares for them, and
- understand the basic truths of the Christian faith, be familiar with Jesus' core teachings, and be introduced to the plan of salvation.

Why Memorize?

We memorize Bible verses to understand them and learn how to apply them in daily life. God doesn't give points for the most verses memorized. His interest lies in whether we follow what those verses say. As you read this book to your children, take time to talk about what each passage means and how it can help them. It is far more important that they understand the meaning of a verse than that they get all the words exactly right.

Explain that Jesus memorized Scripture, too. He quoted Old Testament Scripture when He faced Satan's temptation, when He taught, and when He defended the truth. Your children will also face temptations and difficult situations. This is why they memorize—to have God's Word in their hearts and to learn to live the way He wants them to—the best way.

How to Memorize?

First, use everyday situations. Take every opportunity to show your children how these verses apply. If they are afraid at night, turn to a verse about God's love or His always being with them. This imprints the verse on their minds and connects it to real life.

Second, repetition is a great learning tool. Every child has a favorite book he or she loves to hear read over and over. Soon, the child is "reading" that book to the parent—from memory. It will be the same with this book. Your children will soon be telling you what it says. Try reading the book through a couple of times using all the text, without stopping to follow the tips. Then read, stopping to use the tips and memorize the verses. Later, read only the memory verses. This kind of repetition aids memorization and helps your children grasp the whole picture of God's story.

Third, each verse comes with a tip for memorizing it. Some tips are a simple statement such as a suggestion to play "Pop-Up Verse." Others point to a larger activity, puzzle, or song in the back of the book. On your third or fourth read through the book, take the time to act on these tips, doing the puzzles or activities together. If these activities seem too difficult for your child, turn to the "Miscellaneous Memorization Tips" in the back for an alternate activity. These enjoyable tools for memorization take a little preparation and time. They can be used to help your children memorize a variety of verses. If you use them, consider getting a "Memory Aid Box" in which to keep the puzzles, cards, and various aids that you prepare. That way you will have them handy for review or to reuse with another child.

Above all, make the process *fun*! As you do the puzzles together, eat a favorite snack, listen to music that relates to the topic, do a painting, or even paint yourselves! Make the process into a game by adding actions or changing body positions. The goal is to help your children look forward to learning the next verse.

You might want to begin with the "Books of the Bible" song on pages 132–135. This will familiarize your children with the names and order of the books that are the source of the verses they are about to memorize.

Finally, consider preparing a progress chart that can serve as an incentive. On your chart, list the memory verses with check-off boxes for each child. When the child memorizes a verse, make an event out of checking off the relevant box. When all the verses are memorized, celebrate with a party.

You're ready. Enjoy!

God Made Everything

"In the beginning, God created the heavens and the earth." GENESIS 1:1

God made the stars and planets, the sun and moon. He made everything in the universe, big and small. He made everything that lives on the earth: animals and plants, fish and birds, bugs and butterflies.

It was all very good.

Tip: Ask a series of simple questions about the verse and have the child answer. For example: "When was everything created?" (In the beginning.) "Who created it?" (God.) "What did He create?" (The heavens and the earth.)

God
Made You

"So God created the human race; in the image of God He created it; male and female He created them." GENESIS 1:27

The first people were Adam and Eve. They lived in the garden of Eden and had a wonderful life with God. God loved Adam and Eve just like He loves us. He wanted them to obey Him because He was their Father in heaven and He knew what was best for them.

Tip: Play "Pop-Up Verse." Sit on a chair or the bed and take turns saying a word from the verse. As you say your word stand up then sit right back down again.

Don't Eat from the Tree!

"Then the LORD God gave the man a command, 'You may freely eat from any tree of the garden, but from the tree of knowledge of good and evil you must not eat, for the day you eat from it, you will certainly die.'"
GENESIS 2:16–17

Satan was God's enemy. He didn't want Adam and Eve to obey God and be His children. So Satan appeared as a snake and lied to them. Then Adam and Eve ate from the forbidden tree. They sinned by disobeying God. So God sent them away from the garden. But God still loved them. He had a plan for them to be forgiven for their sins. Years later, He would send Jesus to pay for sin, so people could live forever with God.

Tip: See the activity on page 136.

Noah and
the Ark

The number of people on earth grew and grew.
The people would not listen to God or obey
Him. The world became a very bad place. But
God found one man named Noah who loved
Him. God told Noah to build a big boat, called
an ark.

> *"The LORD then said to Noah, 'Enter the
> ark, you and all your household, for I have
> regarded you alone as righteous in my sight
> among this generation.'"* GENESIS 7:1

To show people that sin was very bad, God sent
a huge flood to destroy the world. But everyone
in the ark was saved.

Tip: Have your children imagine the verse: the huge boat;
Noah—the only man who loves God—entering with his
family; storm clouds brewing; bad people ("this genera-
tion") laughing at them.

Nothing Is Too Hard for God

Many years later, God chose Abraham and Sarah to be part of His plan. They would be the parents of His chosen people. One day Jesus would be born into this family.

Now Abraham and Sarah were very old, with no children. Sarah wondered if God could still give her a son. God said,

> *"Is anything too difficult for the LORD? I will return to you at the appointed time, about this time next year, and Sarah will have a son."* GENESIS 18:14

Tip: Repeat the verse to your child, leaving out the last word, then the second-last word, and so on. Your child fills in the missing word(s) until he/she can say the entire verse.

Abraham Believed

God kept His promise to Sarah. A year later she had a son named Isaac.

God told Abraham that he would be the father and grandfather of so many people that he wouldn't be able to count them all.

> *"[Abraham] believed in the LORD, and He credited it to him as righteousness."*
> GENESIS 15:6

God also promised that He would give the land Abraham was living in to his family to be their home. It would be a place where they would be safe. They would live with God there and follow Him and learn about Him.

Tip: See the activity on page 137.

A Great Nation

God told Abraham:

> *"I will make you into a great nation, bless you and make your name great; so you will be a blessing. I will bless those who bless you, but whoever curses you I will curse. All the families of the earth will be blessed by you."* GENESIS 12:2–3

This was God's plan. After Abraham's family became a nation, God would bless everyone by sending Jesus to be born into this family.

Isaac's son Jacob, also called Israel, had 12 sons who all had big families. They moved to Egypt, grew into a great nation, then became slaves. After many years, God chose someone to take them home to the land He had promised Abraham.

Tip: Put actions to words: thumbs up for "bless" and down for "curse," march for "nation," point for "you" and "I."

Face
to Face

God chose Moses to help His people, the Israelites, get home. Moses was not sure he could lead the people, but he did everything God told him to do. Moses became a great man. God had a special relationship with him.

> *"The LORD would speak with Moses face to face as a man speaks to his friend."*
> EXODUS 33:11A

Moses told Pharaoh, king of Egypt, to let God's people go. Finally, Pharaoh agreed, and Moses led Abraham's family, the nation of Israel, toward the land God had promised them.

Tip: Put your face close to your child's and take turns saying the words of the verse. You say the first word, he or she says the second, and so on.

24

Humble
Moses

Moses led God's people into the desert. God showed them that He could take care of them there. He saved them from the Egyptians at the Red Sea. He guided them by day and night. He helped Moses do many amazing miracles for them.

Moses humbly trusted God and told everyone God was the real miracle-worker.

"Now Moses was a very humble man, more so than anyone on the face of the earth."
NUMBERS 12:3

Tip: Go over the verse several times. Then throw something (teddy bear or sock) into the air. See how many words of the verse your child can say before you catch the object again. Have your child try to improve each time.

Compassionate God

Moses wanted to know God better. God wanted Moses to know Him too so that Moses could teach the people about Him. So God called Moses up to the top of a mountain and told Moses what He was like.

> *"The LORD passed in front of him and proclaimed, 'The LORD, the LORD, a compassionate and gracious God, slow to anger and abundant in love and faithfulness.'"*
> EXODUS 34:6

Tip: Ask simple questions about the verse such as: "What did the Lord do?" (The Lord passed in front of him and proclaimed [said something].) "Who is compassionate?" (The Lord, the Lord.) "What kind of God is He?" (Compassionate and gracious.) "He's slow to what?" (Anger.) "What is He abundant in?" (Love and faithfulness.)

The Ten Commandments

While Moses was on the mountain, God gave him rules and guidelines called the Ten Commandments. These rules would help the people know how to live good lives.

> *"You shall have no other gods before Me.*
> *You shall not make an idol for yourself.*
> *You shall not misuse the name of the LORD*
>   *your God.*
> *Remember to keep the Sabbath day holy.*
> *Honor your father and your mother.*
> *You shall not murder.*
> *You shall not commit adultery.*
> *You shall not steal.*
> *You shall not bear false witness.*
> *You shall not covet."*
> EXODUS 20:3–17 SUMMARIZED

Tip: See activity on pages 138–139.

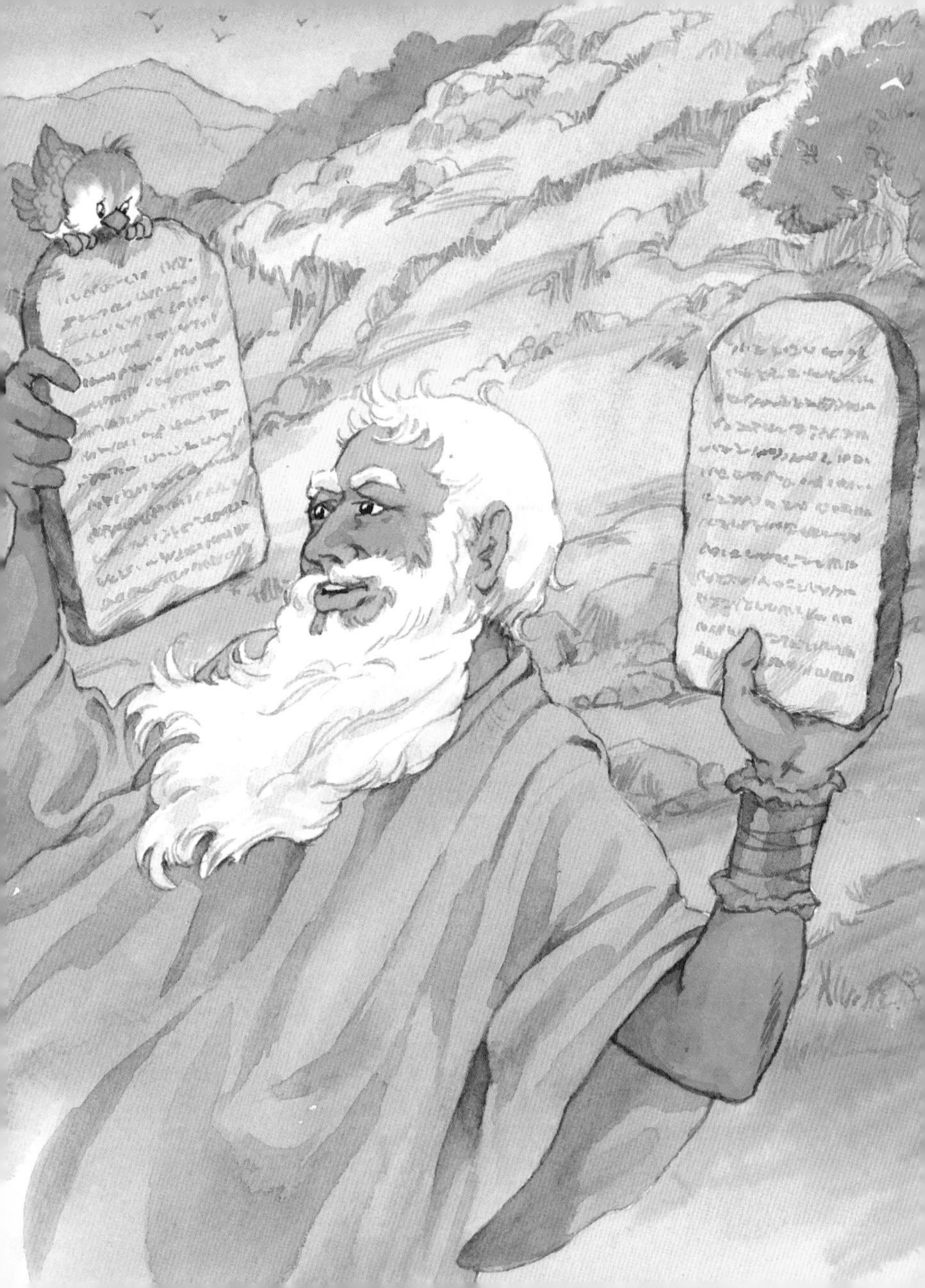

The Blessing

God wanted the people of Israel to know He loved them and would look after them. He told Aaron the priest to bless them, saying,

> *"May the LORD bless and protect you. May the LORD make his face shine on you and be gracious to you. May the LORD look kindly on you and give you peace."*
> NUMBERS 6:24–26

When the Israelites were ready to enter the promised land, God told Moses to choose a new leader for them. Moses was an old man and could not go with them.

Tip: Clap out the rhythm. For the first thing in each phrase that God does, clap to the right. For each phrase's second thing, clap to the left.

Be Strong and Courageous

After Moses died, Joshua became the new Israelite leader. God encouraged him saying,

> *"But be strong and very courageous to persevere in observing all that My servant Moses commanded you. Do not turn away from it to the right or the left, so that you will have success wherever you go."*
> JOSHUA 1:7

Joshua led the Israelites into the promised land and defeated the sinful people there.

God kept His promise to Abraham and gave his family a safe home. Now God could really teach them about Himself!

Tip: Come up with actions for key words (such as flexing muscles for "strong," jumping high for "courageous"). Talk about the words' meanings as you do. Say the verse with the actions until you can do it by heart.

I'll Go Where You Go

Many years after the Israelites entered the promised land, a woman named Naomi moved with her family to a nearby country. After her husband and sons died, Naomi returned home with her daughter-in-law Ruth. Ruth said,

"Wherever you go, I will go, and wherever you stay, I will stay; your people will be my people, and your God will be my God."
RUTH 1:16B

God chose Ruth and her husband Boaz for His plan. Their son Obed became the grandfather of David. Jesus would be born into David's family.

Tip: Act it out. Pretend to send "Ruth" back. Ruth follows, saying the first part of the verse. When you stay, she stays, saying the words. Use a family picture for "your people" and a Bible for "your God."

God Looks Inside

Years later, God's people wanted a king. God gave them Saul as king, but Saul disobeyed God. So God sent His prophet Samuel to Ruth's grandson Jesse to choose a new king. This new king would obey God because he loved Him.

Samuel thought Jesse's eldest son looked like he would make a good king, but God said,

> *"The LORD doesn't see as people see. For people look at the outer appearance, but the LORD looks at the heart."* 1 SAMUEL 16:7B

Tip: See the activity on page 140.

A Man After God's Heart

God chose David, Jesse's youngest son, to lead His people. When the time was right, God removed Saul as king.

> *"After removing him, He raised up David as their king, of whom he testified: 'I have found David the son of Jesse, a man after my heart, who will carry out all My will.'"*
> ACTS 13:22

David became the greatest king God's people ever had. He loved God and followed Him with his whole heart.

In God's plan, David would show God's people how to obey God. He would also help them know God better and understand His love.

Tip: Repeat the verse using two voices, your regular voice for the narration and a very deep one for God's words. Have your child do the same.

Shepherd's Psalm

David praised God by writing songs and playing the harp.

"The LORD is my shepherd, I lack nothing. He makes me lie down in green meadows; He leads me beside calm waters. He refreshes my life; He leads me in paths of righteousness for the sake of His name. Even when I walk through the darkest valley, I will fear no harm because You are with me; Your rod and Your staff comfort me.

"You set a table before me in the sight of my enemies; You anoint my head with oil; My cup is filled to the brim. Certainly, goodness and mercy will pursue me all the days of my life, and I will dwell in the house of the LORD for the rest of my life."
PSALM 23

Tip: Help your children imagine this wonderful picture. Have them describe things that remind them of this verse.

Get
Wisdom

David's son Solomon became king after him. He was the wisest king ever. He knew that wisdom helped people live in a way that pleased God. He said,

"The first principle about wisdom is: Get wisdom! Whatever it costs you, get understanding!" PROVERBS 4:7

But the people didn't listen. They were foolish instead of wise and kept disobeying God.

Tip: Divide the verse into its four phrases plus the reference. Make up mimes to represent each phrase; for example, hold up a finger for "first principle" and point to your head for "wisdom," search until you "get" wisdom, empty your pockets, paying out big bucks, have an "a-ha!" experience as you "understand." Put them together, saying the words. Repeat until your child has memorized the verse.

Choose
Life

God wanted to bless His people with good things, but they kept making bad choices. He sent messengers to warn them about what would happen if they kept disobeying Him. One messenger said,

"Today I call heaven and earth to witness against you: I have set before you life or death, blessing or curse. Choose life, so that you and your descendants will live."
DEUTERONOMY 30:19

Choosing life meant choosing to love and obey God. But the people kept on choosing to do the wrong thing. They kept on sinning.

Tip: See activity on page 141.

God Has Plans

God loved the Israelites even though they disobeyed. When they kept disobeying, God let their enemies take many of them away to Babylon. God's prophet, Jeremiah, sent a message telling them how God wanted them to live. He said when they prayed to God and chose to love and obey Him, they would return home and do well. God had good things planned for them.

> *"For I know the plans that I have in mind for you, declares the LORD—plans for peace and not for disaster, to give you a hopeful future."* JEREMIAH 29:11

Tip: Toss something (a pillow or a toy) back and forth from your lap to your child's as you say the verse. Whoever has the object says the next word of the verse.

Good
Daniel

Daniel was one of the people taken to Babylon by his enemy. God made him a leader there. Daniel's enemies tried to find him making mistakes to get him in trouble. But Daniel didn't do anything wrong.

> *"No negligence or corruption was found in him."* DANIEL 6:4B

So Daniel's enemies made a law that no one could pray to God. Daniel loved God and prayed anyway. For punishment he was thrown into a lions' den. God protected him by shutting the lions' mouths.

Tip: Help your children imagine this. Daniel works hard and does all his chores. Describe how carefully he would work. Daniel's enemies watch him, trying to find fault. But even if they surprise him or sneak around, they can't find him doing anything wrong.

Esther's Days

A few years later, a faithful man named Mordecai told his young Jewish cousin, Esther, *"Perhaps you have become queen for such a time as this"* (ESTHER 4:14D). Before she was even born, God had special plans for Esther. An evil leader in Persia wanted to destroy God's people. But God made Esther queen just in time to save them.

Esther knew King David was right when he said,

> *"Your eyes saw me before I was born; all the days You planned for me were written in Your book before the first one began."*
> PSALM 139:16

With His people safe, God got ready for the next part of His plan—sending Jesus!

Tip: Have your child throw an object (beanbag, ball) through a hoop or into a container. When the child succeeds, he or she says the verse and scores a point. When the score is three, celebrate with a treat or big hug.

You'll Have a Son

God chose a young girl named Mary to be the mother of a very special baby: His own Son. Mary and her husband Joseph would raise Jesus.

> *"She will give birth to a son, and you are to name Him Jesus, because He will save His people from their sins."* MATTHEW 1:21

Long ago God had promised to send someone to save people from their sins and make things right between people and God. God kept His promise. Jesus was that person. He would pay for everyone's sins so they could be God's children. And God would be their Father in heaven.

Tip: See the activity on page 142–143.

Jesus Is Born

While Mary was pregnant, she and Joseph had to travel to Bethlehem to be counted in a census. The town was crowded. All rooms were full so Mary and Joseph had to stay in a stable.

"While they were there, it happened that the days were completed for her to give birth. Then she gave birth to her firstborn Son, and she wrapped Him snugly in cloth and laid Him in a manger—because there was no room for them at the inn." LUKE 2:6–7

God was very happy because, just as He planned, His Son was born. He sent angels to tell shepherds the good news. God's big plan was going ahead!

Tip: Ask simple questions about the verse: When did it happen? What days were completed? Who did she give birth to? How did she wrap Him? Where did she lay Him? Why?

Jesus Grows Up

As Jesus grew up, He obeyed His parents, did His chores, and learned about God's Word.

"Jesus increased in wisdom and stature, and in favor with God and with people."
LUKE 2:52

When Jesus was twelve years old, He went with His parents to the temple in Jerusalem. He listened to the teachers there and talked with them. Everyone was amazed at how much He understood about God.

Tip: Play "Pop-Up Verse." Sit on a chair or the bed and take turns saying a word from the verse. As you say your word stand up then sit right back down again. Or start out standing and play "Pop-Down Verse."

This Is
My Son

At the age of 30, Jesus was ready to begin telling people about His Father, who is God, and God's kingdom. But first, Jesus went to John the Baptist to be baptized. He wanted to do everything God's way.

"After Jesus was baptized, He went up immediately from the water. The heavens suddenly opened for Him, and He saw the Spirit of God descending like a dove and coming down on Him. And there came a voice from heaven: This is My beloved Son. I take delight in Him!" MATTHEW 3:16–17

Jesus' Father in heaven wanted everyone to know how happy He was with Jesus.

Tip: Repeat the verse using a very expressive voice that shows how amazing it was. Use a very deep voice for God's words. Have your child do the same.

Fishers of Men

Part of God's plan was for Jesus to teach others how to serve and follow Him. So Jesus chose some men to be His disciples, or special students. He found two brothers, Peter and Andrew, throwing their fishing nets into the lake, trying to catch fish.

"'Follow Me,' Jesus told them, 'and I will make you into fishers of men!'" MARK 1:17

So they left their nets and followed Jesus. They lived and traveled with Jesus, learning about God and His kingdom.

Tip: Act the verse out as you repeat it. Pretend to fish.

Twelve Disciples

The twelve ordinary men Jesus chose to be His disciples followed Him and learned from Him.

> *"Simon, whom He also named Peter, and*
> *Andrew his brother;*
> *James and John;*
> *Philip and Bartholomew;*
> *Matthew and Thomas;*
> *James the son of Alphaeus, and Simon*
> *called the Zealot;*
> *Judas the son of James, and Judas Iscariot,*
> *who became a traitor."* LUKE 6:14–16

They spent almost every day for three years with Jesus, learning about God.

Tip: See the song "Twelve Guys" on pages 144–145. The names are in a slightly different order but the song will help your children learn the disciples' names.

Jesus' Work

Jesus set about doing the work God sent Him to do.

> *"Jesus was going all over Galilee, teaching in their synagogues, preaching the good news of the kingdom, and healing every disease and sickness among the people."* MATTHEW 4:23

Jesus showed people that God cared about their needs. He wanted them to know how much God loved them. He also wanted them to follow God's commands. He knew that was the best thing for them.

Tip: Divide the verse into phrases, with the reference. Say the phrases out of order and have your child identify which phrase should be first, second, third, etc. (You might want to leave the first phrase first.) Do this several times, changing the order.

The Blesseds

People followed Jesus and His disciples everywhere they went. Jesus wanted the people to know the best way to live. So He taught:

> *"Blessed are the poor in spirit, because the kingdom of heaven is theirs.*
> *Blessed are those who mourn, because they will be comforted.*
> *Blessed are the gentle, because they will inherit the earth.*
> *Blessed are those who hunger and thirst for righteousness, because they will be filled.*
> *Blessed are the merciful, because they will be shown mercy.*
> *Blessed are the pure in heart, because they will see God.*
> *Blessed are the peacemakers, because they will be called sons of God.*
> *Blessed are those who are persecuted for righteousness, because the kingdom of heaven is theirs."* MATTHEW 5:3–10

Tip: Play "That's Not What It Says." (See pages 138–139 for the game instructions.)

Love Your Enemies

Jesus taught the people many things about how to live. What He taught often surprised people. But it was the best way to live because it was God's way.

> *"But I say to you who listen: Love your enemies, do good to those who hate you, bless those who curse you, pray for those who mistreat you. If anyone hits you on the cheek, offer the other also. And if anyone takes away your coat, don't hold back your shirt either."* LUKE 6:27–29

Jesus wanted us to love everyone just as God loves us. He was saying we are to love and treat people well, no matter how they treat us.

Tip: See the activity on pages 146–147.

The Lord's Prayer

Jesus also taught people how to pray.

"Therefore, you should pray like this:
Our Father in heaven,
Your name be honored as holy.
Your kingdom come.
Your will be done
on earth as it is in heaven.
Give us today our daily bread.
And forgive us our debts,
as we also have forgiven our debtors.
And do not bring us into temptation,
but deliver us from the evil one.
For Yours is the kingdom
and the power
and the glory forever,
Amen." MATTHEW 6:9–13

Tip: Leave out words at the end of the prayer and have your child fill them in. Omit more words each time until your child says the whole prayer.

Seek the Kingdom

Jesus knew people were concerned about clothes, food, money, jobs, and how they looked. He told them these were the wrong things to worry about. Jesus said if they focused on the right things, they wouldn't need to worry about those other things. He said,

"Seek first the kingdom of God and His righteousness, and all these things will be provided for you." MATTHEW 6:33

Jesus meant that we should think about God first, want Him most, and trust Him to take care of all the other things.

Tip: Come up with a simple rhythm to clap to this verse. Ask, "Can you say the verse while clapping your hands?" Have the child do it. "While jumping up and down?" "While patting your head?" Use a variety of physical actions while saying the verse.

Lost or Found?

Jesus wanted everyone to know that God is so important that they need to be willing to give up everything for Him. Then they will find that they have won instead of lost!

"Anyone finding his life will lose it, and anyone losing his life because of Me will find it." MATTHEW 10:39

Jesus was saying that if we believe in Him and make Him more important than anything else in our lives, we will live forever in heaven.

Tip: Say the verse a few times. Ask your child to listen closely as you repeat the verse omitting a word (or words) from the middle. Have the child "find" the missing word in his/her memory. Repeat, omitting additional words from various places, until the child can "find" the entire verse without help.

Do to Others

God loves us and wants us to be happy. One of the things that makes us happy is good friendships. So Jesus gave us advice about getting along.

"Just as you want others to do for you, do the same for them." LUKE 6:31

If we do this, we will be good friends and have good friends.

Tip: Use something your child likes, such as a favorite teddy bear. Throw the teddy to the child "giving" it to him or her. Say the verse. Have the child throw the teddy to you "as he/she wants you to do for him/her" and say the verse. After each repetition, ask your child for a way he/she wants to be treated and can treat others. Or ask for qualities and actions of good friends. Do this until the child knows the verse.

Jesus
Is God

Jesus was so different that people wondered who He really was. Some thought He was a prophet. Jesus asked His disciples who they thought He was.

"Simon Peter answered, 'You are the Messiah, the Son of the living God!'"
MATTHEW 16:16

Peter was exactly right. Jesus was the One who God had told Adam and Eve about long ago. He was the One who would pay for our sins and make things right between God and us. He would help us be God's children.

Tip: Take turns saying words from the verse. You say the first, your child says the second, you say the third, etc. Then let your child say the first word while you say the second, and so on.

Small Faith

Jesus did many miracles like healing people who were sick and feeding thousands of people with hardly any food. The disciples were amazed. Jesus told them they could do amazing things too, if they had even a tiny bit of faith.

> *"For I assure you: If you have faith the size of a mustard seed, you will tell this mountain, 'Move from here to there,' and it will move. Nothing will be impossible for you."* MATTHEW 17:20b

A small mustard seed grows into a large bush. Believing and trusting God even a little has big effects.

Tip: This is a good verse to have your children imagine. Have them imagine a tiny seed beside a big mountain. Then have them imagine themselves, small beside the mountain, with a little faith, telling the mountain to move. It does!

Children, Come!

Children loved Jesus and wanted to be around Him. But the disciples thought Jesus was too busy. They sent the children away.

"Then Jesus said, 'Leave the children alone, and don't try to keep them from coming to Me, because the kingdom of heaven is made up of people like this.'" MATTHEW 19:14

Jesus loved children. He hugged and blessed them.

Tip: Repeat the verse several times. Then throw something (beach ball or balloon) into the air. How much of the verse can your child say before you catch it (or, if it's a balloon, hit it up again)? On the second throw, the child continues from where he or she left off. How many throws does it take to finish the verse?

The Greatest Commandments

One day a man asked Jesus what the most important commandment was.

> *["Jesus] said to him, 'You shall love the Lord your God with all your heart, with all your soul, and with all your mind.' This is the greatest and most important commandment. The second is like it: 'You shall love your neighbor as yourself.' All the Law and the Prophets depend on these two commandments."* MATTHEW 22:37–40

If we are careful to always keep these commandments, our lives will please God. Keeping them properly helps us keep the rest of God's laws too.

Tip: See the activity on pages 148–149.

Jesus Is
the Way

Jesus began telling His disciples that He would soon be going away, back to His Father. This made them very sad. They didn't want Jesus to leave. He said they knew the way to where He was going. But Thomas wasn't so sure.

> *"Jesus told him, I am the way, the truth, and the life. No one comes to the Father except through Me."* JOHN 14:6

The only way to God is by believing and following Jesus.

Tip: Play "That's Not What It Says." (See pages 138–139 for the game instructions.) For example, you might use words like "I am the *gate*, the *vineyard*, and the *altar*. No *temple* comes to the Father *after chasing* Me."

88

The Holy Spirit

Jesus knew that the disciples would need help and encouragement after He went away. He promised that He would not leave them alone.

> *"But the Counselor, the Holy Spirit, whom the Father will send in My name, will teach you all things and remind you of everything I have told you."* JOHN 14:26

The Holy Spirit, God's Spirit, would live in the hearts of those who believe in Jesus. He would always be with them, helping them follow Jesus and live God's way.

Tip: Put the words of the verse into a familiar tune like "Climb Up Sunshine Mountain" or your own tune. Beat out the rhythm with your hands as you repeat the verse.

Jesus' Friends

Jesus loved His disciples very much. He said:

"You are My friends if you do what I command you." JOHN 15:14

It was so simple! If they obeyed the things Jesus taught, they would always have a close relationship with Him.

We can have a close relationship with Jesus too. We just need to believe in Him and follow His commandments.

Tip: Have your child throw an object (ball, rolled up shirt, slipper) through a hoop or into a container. Upon succeeding, the child says the verse and scores a point. When the score is three, celebrate with a treat or a big hug.

Jesus Is Crucified

Jesus had done the work God sent Him to do. It was time for God's plan to be fulfilled. Jesus would pay for everyone's sin and make a way for people to be God's children and live forever with Him. He said,

> *"The Son of Man [Jesus] must be betrayed into the hands of sinful men, be crucified, and rise on the third day."* LUKE 24:7

That's exactly what happened. Judas Iscariot betrayed Jesus, and Jesus' enemies killed Him on a cross. Jesus didn't deserve to die: He died to pay for *our* sins.

But that wasn't the end.

Tip: Go over the verse a few times. Then say it, omitting a word or two from the middle. Have your child tell you what is missing. Repeat, omitting different (and more) words each time.

Jesus Is Risen

Jesus' friends put His body into a tomb. On the third day some women visited the tomb. They wanted to put special burial spices on Jesus' body. They met an angel there. The angel said,

> *"He is not here! For He has been resurrected, just as He said. Come and see the place where He lay."* MATTHEW 28:6

The tomb was empty! Jesus was alive!

Jesus appeared to His disciples several times, helping them understand what had happened. He explained how He had risen from the tomb and fulfilled God's plan.

Tip: Act it out. The closet is Jesus' tomb. You, Jesus' friend, search for Him. Your child, the angel, says with words and gestures that Jesus isn't here but has risen. He/she invites you to see where He lay.

God Loved the World

From the beginning God's plan was for Jesus to show us what God is like, teach us how much He cares and how He wants us to live, then die to pay for our sins so we could have eternal life. That means that because Jesus fulfilled God's plan, we can be God's children and live with Him forever!

"For God loved the world in this way: He gave His only Son, so that everyone who believes in Him will not perish but have eternal life." JOHN 3:16

Tip: See the activity on page 150.

Open the Door

Jesus wants to be part of everyone's life. He is waiting for us to open our hearts to Him.

"Listen! I stand at the door and knock. If anyone hears My voice and opens the door, I will come in to him and have dinner with him, and he with Me." REVELATION 3:20

When we invite Jesus in, He comes and lives in our hearts. He always loves us and helps us follow God and do what's right.

Tip: Act it out. Let your child be Jesus knocking at the door, saying the verse. When you hear "His" voice, open the door and let "Jesus" in. Have a snack together to represent dinner.

Speak It Out

When you believe in Jesus you need to say it out loud.

"If you confess with your mouth, 'Jesus is Lord,' and believe in your heart that God raised Him from the dead, you will be saved." ROMANS 10:9

Then you belong to Jesus. He will look after you and live in your heart. He will help you know what to do and say to live well and have the best life you can.

Tip: Ready for some exercise? Say the first phrase from a sitting position. Then stand to shout, "Jesus is Lord!" Sit for the next phrase and stand for "God raised Him from the dead!" Sit for the final phrase. Stand for the reference.

The Great Commission

Before Jesus returned to heaven, He gave His followers a big job to do while He was gone.

> *"Go, therefore, and make disciples of all nations, baptizing them in the name of the Father and of the Son and of the Holy Spirit, teaching them to observe everything I have commanded you. And remember, I am with you always, to the end of the age."*
> MATTHEW 28:19–20

God's plan is still going on. Part of it is for everyone in the world to hear about what Jesus did so they know that they can be God's children. Telling everyone this wonderful news is a job for all God's followers!

Tip: See the activity on page 151.

Go Forward

After Jesus returned to heaven, many other people helped with the job of telling others the good news of what Jesus had done. One helper was Paul. He loved Jesus very much. Paul said,

> *"One thing I do: forgetting what is behind and reaching forward to what is ahead, I pursue as my goal the prize promised by God's heavenly call in Christ Jesus."*
> PHILIPPIANS 3:13B–14

Paul meant that following God was the most important thing in his life.

Tip: Put this to a familiar tune using a question/answer format. For example, *You*: "One thing I do. What do I do?" *Children*: "Forget what's behind!" *You*: "And reaching forward. What do I reach for?" *Children*: "What's ahead." And so on through the verse.

Love

Paul taught that the most important thing for Jesus' followers to learn is how to love one another. He also taught people what real love is like.

> *"Love is patient; love is kind. Love does not envy; is not boastful; is not conceited; does not act improperly; is not selfish; is not provoked; does not keep a record of wrongs; finds no joy in unrighteousness, but rejoices in the truth; bears all things, believes all things, hopes all things, endures all things. Love never ends. But as for prophecies, they will come to an end; as for languages, they will cease; as for knowledge, it will come to an end."* 1 CORINTHIANS 13:4–8

Tip: See activity on pages 152–153.

Fruit of
the Spirit

Paul wrote letters to new believers to help them know what being a Christian was all about. He told them that God's Spirit was working in their lives, making them into the kind of people God wanted them to be. He wrote,

> *"The fruit of the Spirit is love, joy, peace, patience, kindness, goodness, faith, gentleness, self-control. Against such things there is no law."* GALATIANS 5:22–23

When people grow with God's Spirit, soon these things are seen in their lives and friendships. It's God's good fruit growing in them.

Tip: See the song on page 154. It uses "faithfulness" instead of "faith," but it will help your children learn what the Spirit grows in us.

Be Kind

God wants us to have good friendships and treat each other well. So Paul wrote to Christians to tell them how to act toward one another. He said,

> *"Be kind and compassionate to one another, forgiving one another, just as God also forgave you in Christ."* EPHESIANS 4:32

We need to always treat people kindly. And when we have arguments or get hurt, we need to forgive each other and make things right.

Tip: Say the verse using synonyms for key words. For example, "Be *nice* and *loving* to *everyone* . . ." Replace one word each time through. Have your children tell you which word is the synonym and then supply the correct one.

Obey Your Parents

Paul taught about families, too. He told parents how to love each other and how to treat their children. And he said,

> *"Children, obey your parents in the Lord, because this is right."* EPHESIANS 6:1

God promises to bless children who honor and respect their parents by obeying them. When you do this, Ephesians 6:3 says *"that it may go well with you and that you may have a long life in the land."*

Tip: Put this verse to a familiar tune. Intersperse questions. For example, after "Children, obey your parents in the Lord. . . ." you might shout, "Why do you obey?" Your children answer, in rhythm, "Because this is right." Or you sing, "Children, who do you obey?" "Your parents in the Lord."

Be
Happy

Paul had many troubles, but he never let them get him down. Even when he was in prison for being a Christian he wrote about being happy.

"Rejoice always! Pray constantly. Give thanks in everything, for this is God's will for you in Christ Jesus." 1 Thessalonians 5:16–18

Paul knew that God was in control and could work everything out for the best. Paul trusted God and told us we should trust God, too.

Tip: Take turns saying the words of the verse. You say the first word, your child says the second and so on. For a change, say two words each, then three, then four.

God's Word

God chose special people to write down His words so we would know His plan, what He was like, and how He wanted us to live. He made sure the Bible, called Scripture, said exactly what He wanted. God gave us the Bible so we could learn the truth about Him from its words and so we would know how to be His children and live for Him.

"All Scripture is inspired by God and is profitable for teaching, for rebuking, for correcting, for training in righteousness, so that the man of God may be complete, equipped for every good work." 2 TIMOTHY 3:16–17

God's Word is true! It helps us live well.

Tip: See the activity on page 155.

Meet Together

Christians meet together as the church. At church, they encourage one another and learn about Jesus. Some people think they don't need to go to church. God's Word says, we should love one another and encourage each other,

"Not staying away from our meetings, as some habitually do."
HEBREWS 10:25

Church is God's idea. It helps us grow strong.

Tip: Throw an object (teddy bear or sock) into the air. How much of the verse can your child say before you catch the object? Let the child say the next part of the verse on the second throw. How many throws does it take to say the whole verse and reference? Repeat until the child can say it all during one throw.

Resist
the Devil

God knew we would face trouble. Satan, also called the devil, tricked Adam and Eve and tried to hurt Jesus. He tries to hurt Jesus' followers, too. He still lies, trying to get us to disobey God. But don't worry.

"Submit to God. But resist the Devil, and he will flee from you." JAMES 4:7

When you're God's child and you love and obey Him, He will help you resist temptation and the devil. He will help you do what's right if you ask Him to.

Tip: Go over the verse a few times. Then say the three phrases in a wrong order. Have your child tell you the correct order. Repeat, changing the order each time until your child has it memorized.

God
Forgives

No one except Jesus is perfect. That means we make mistakes and do wrong things. God knows this. He understands.

> *"If we confess our sins, He is faithful and righteous to forgive us our sins and to cleanse us from all unrighteousness."*
> 1 JOHN 1:9

God will help us change and grow.

Tip: Read the verse as it is below, asking your children to replace the words that don't belong in the verse with the right words that mean the same.
　　"If we *admit* our *wrongs*, He is faithful and *fair* to *let us off from* our *disobedient acts* and to *wash* us from *every* unrighteousness." (1 JOHN 1:9)

God
Is Love

Jesus' disciple, John, knew God loved us more than we could understand—because that's just who God is.

> *"And we have come to know and to believe the love that God has for us. God is love, and the one who remains in love remains in God, and God remains in him."* 1 JOHN 4:16

Everything God does comes out of love because He *is* love.

When we follow God and live loving lives, God teaches us even more about love.

Tip: Put actions to key words such as touching your head for "know," touching your heart for "believe," hugging yourself for "love," pointing up for "God," holding up one finger for "one," cradling a baby for "remains."

The Father's House

Jesus is in heaven getting things ready for us to come and be with Him forever. Jesus promised,

"In My Father's house are many dwelling places; if not, I would have told you. I am going away to prepare a place for you. If I go away and prepare a place for you, I will come back and receive you to Myself, so that where I am you may be also." JOHN 14:2–3

Tip: Have your child draw a house. Cut the house out and pass it back and forth. Whoever has the house says the next word in the verse.

No More Tears

Heaven is a wonderful place! In heaven, we will be with our loving Heavenly Father just as He planned all along. Everything will be perfect there.

"He will wipe away every tear from their eyes. Death will exist no longer; grief, crying, and pain will exist no longer, because the previous things have passed away."
REVELATION 21:4

When we are in heaven with God forever as His children, His plan will be completely finished!

Tip: Say the verse, omitting the final word for your child to supply. Each time you say the verse, leave off more of the final words until your child is saying the entire verse.

The Books We Love the Best

key of G

He-y kids of all the rest, these are the books we

love the best. We can sing them one by one.

Come on kids lets have some fun. Ge-ne-sis and Ex-o-dus, Le-

vi-ti-cus, Num - bers, Deu - ter-o - no -my,

Jo-shu- a and Ju - dg-es, Ruth and Sam-u- el, Se-cond Sam-u-

el, Kings, Kings, Chron- i-cles and Chron- i - cles,

Ro - mans, First and Se- cond Cor - in - thi - ans, Ga-

la - tians and E- phe - sians, Phil- ip- pi- ans, Co- lo - si- ans,

Thes - sa - lo - ni- ans, Se- cond Thes - sa - lo - ni - ans,

Fi - rst a-nd Se- cond books of Ti- mo- thy, Ti- tus and Phi - le -

mon, He - brews, and Ja - mes,

First and Se- cond Pe - ter, First and Se - cond and

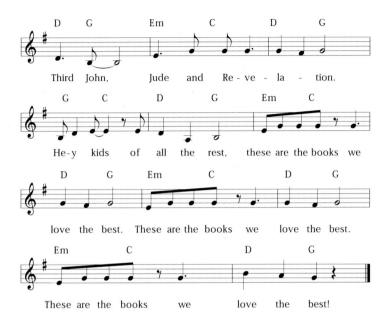

Third John, Jude and Re - ve - la - tion.

He-y kids of all the rest, these are the books we

love the best. These are the books we love the best.

These are the books we love the best!

135

Don't Eat From the Tree!

The memory verse got mixed up with a picture book. Words were replaced with pictures of things that look or sound like the word. Say the words for the pictures to help you learn the memory verse. *(Story found on page 14.)*

"T+🐏 the Lord God gave the 🧔 a 🪮+🧔+d, '🐑📅 fr+🐍+y from any 🌳 of the 🕴+n, but from the 🌳 of know+🛷 of good and evil 🐑 must 🪢+👩 , 4 the day 🐑🐑 from it, 🐑 will certainly ⚰️.'"

Genesis 2 16–17

Abraham Believed

Find and follow the right path that leads through the words of the memory verse to the beautiful land God promised Abraham. *(Story found on page 20.)*

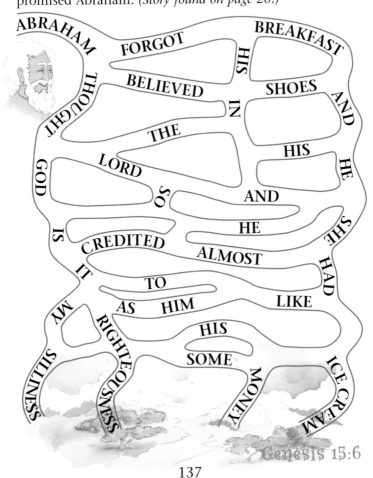

ABRAHAM FORGOT BREAKFAST

THOUGHT BELIEVED HIS SHOES AND

GOD THE IN HIS HE

LORD SO AND

IS CREDITED HE SHE

IT ALMOST HAD

MY AS TO HIM LIKE

SILLINESS RIGHTEOUSNESS HIS SOME MONEY ICE CREAM

Genesis 15:6

The Ten Commandments

(Story found on page 30.)

"That's Not What It Says . . ."

Replace a key word in each commandment with another biblical word. Do this three to four times per commandment, replacing one word each time. For example, "You shall have no *cherubim* before Me." Your child responds, "That's not what it says. It says . . ." and fills in the correct word, repeating the commandment. Then you say, "You shall have no *Passovers* before Me," and again the child responds with the correct commandment.

Here are some possible alternate words you can use:

"You shall have no—*cherubim, Passovers, shepherds' staffs*—before Me.

"You shall not—*climb, weigh, weave*—an—*ark, temple, sheep pen*—for yourself. (e.g. "You shall not *climb* an idol for yourself," then "You shall not make an *ark* for yourself.")

"You shall not—*pray, memorize, cry out*—the—*shekel, lion, Jordan River*—of the Lord your God.

"*Forget, blow a trumpet, lie*—to keep the—*palace, robe, feast*—day—*secret, unclean, for finding sheep.*

"*Sacrifice to, disobey, surprise*—your father and—*Queen Esther, Saint Paul, burning bushes.*

"You shall not—*serve others, have talents, get leprosy.*

"You—*walk to, can if you want, should go home to*—commit—*a miracle, a wedding, laughter.*

"*Sandals, everyone but me, Goliath*—shall not—*use a slingshot, help people, find lost things.*

"You shall not bear false—*weights, lambs, cloaks.*

"You shall not—*look in the mirror, give money away, sing in church.*"

EXODUS 20:3–17 SUMMARIZED

God Looks Inside

The memory verse got mixed up with a picture book again. Words were replaced with pictures of things that look or sound like the word. Say the words for the pictures to help you learn the memory verse. *(Story found on page 38.)*

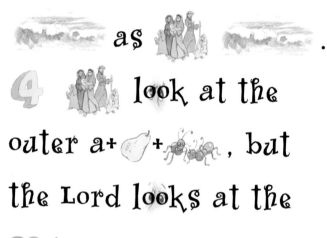

"The Lord doesn't _____ as _____ _____ .
4 _____ look at the outer a + 🍐 + 🐜 , but the Lord looks at the ❤ ."

1 Samuel 16:7B

Choose Life

This memory verse got *very* mixed up with a picture book. You'll have to trade letters in one of the words describing a picture. For example, "(n=c)" means, instead of the "n" in the word, you need to say "c," so "nurse" becomes "curse." *(Story found on page 46.)*

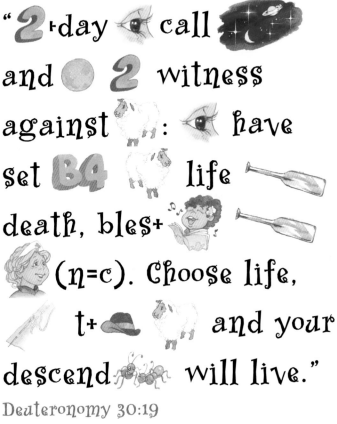

"2·day call and 2 witness against : have set B4 life death, bles+ (n=c). Choose life, t+ and your descend will live."

Deuteronomy 30:19

You'll Have a Son

Find your way through the maze to the reference by following the path connecting the words of the memory verse. Watch out for wrong paths with wrong words! *(Story found on page 54.)*

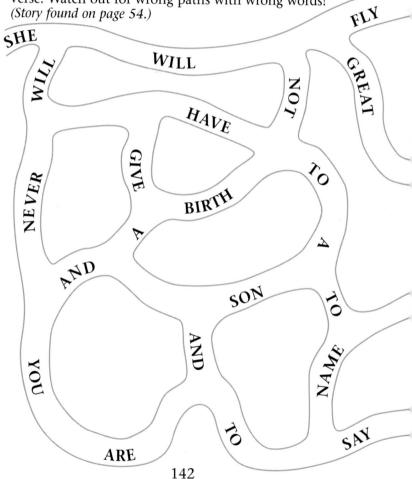

SHE
FLY
WILL
WILL
NOT
GREAT
HAVE
GIVE
NEVER
TO
BIRTH
A
NAME
AND
SON
TO
YOU
AND
NAME
TO
ARE
SAY

142

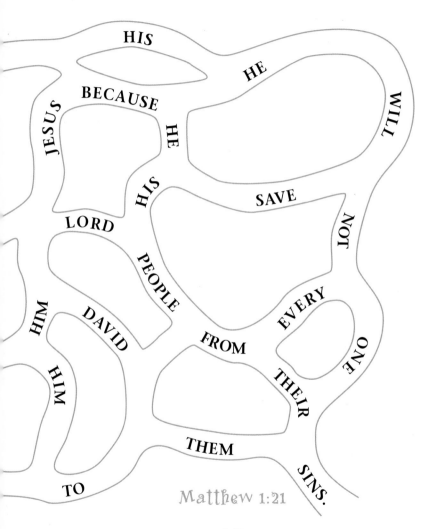

HIS

HE

WILL

JESUS

BECAUSE

HE

LORD

HIS

SAVE

NOT

HIM

PEOPLE

EVERY

DAVID

FROM

ONE

HIM

THEIR

THEM

TO

SINS.

Matthew 1:21

143

Twelve Disciples

Twelve Guys

key of D

Twelve guys or - di - na - ry guys.

Some of them sim - ple and some of them wise.

Twelve guys, or - di - na - ry guys. They were

Je - sus' cho - sen dis - ci - ples.

1. First there was Pe - ter, An - drew, Ja - mes and John.
2. Phi - lip was the cau - tious one and he'd ques - tion you.
3. Ju - das not the trai - tor and James the Less,
4. Peter, Andrew, Ja - mes and John,

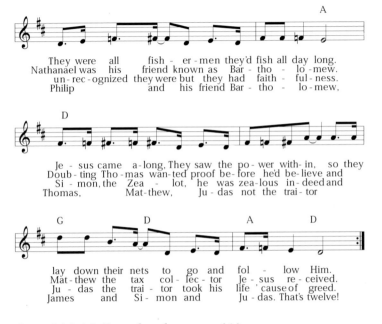

They were   all   fish - er - men they'd fish all day long.
Nathanael was   his   friend known as   Bar - tho -   lo -mew.
un - rec - ognized they were but   they had   faith -   ful - ness.
Philip   and   his friend Bar - tho -   lo - mew,

Je - sus came   a - long, They saw the po - wer with - in,   so they
Doub - ting Tho - mas wan - ted proof be - fore   he'd be - lieve and
Si - mon, the   Zea -   lot,   he was zea - lous in - deed and
Thomas,   Mat - thew,   Ju - das not the trai - tor

lay down their nets   to   go and   fol -   low   Him.
Mat - thew the   tax   col - lec - tor   Je - sus   re - ceived.
Ju - das the   trai - tor took his   life ' cause of   greed.
James   and   Si - mon and   Ju - das. That's twelve!

Luke 6:14–16 *(Story found on page 64.)*

145

Love Your Enemies

Follow the lines from the actions or attitudes on the left to those on the right to learn how God wants you to respond to people. For example, follow the line from "love your" to find out who you should love: "enemies." *(Story found on page 70.)*

But I say to you who listen: Love your

do good to those who

bless those who

pray for those who

If anyone hits you on the cheek,

And if anyone takes away your coat,

curse you,

don't hold back
your shirt either.

enemies,

mistreat you.

offer the
other also.

hate you,

The Greatest Commandments

Once again the verse got mixed up with a picture book and the letters got confused. You'll have to say the words for the pictures or signs and replace some letters. If you're not sure what the pictures are, ask your parents for help. *(Story found on page 86.)*

["Jesus] said to him, '

shall  ♥ the Lord U+r

God with 🪛 U+r ♥

with  🪛 U+r s+🦉,

and with 🪛 U+r 🪨.

This is the 🧀+est and

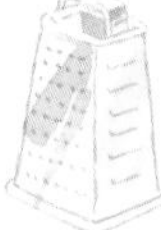

most import+🐜

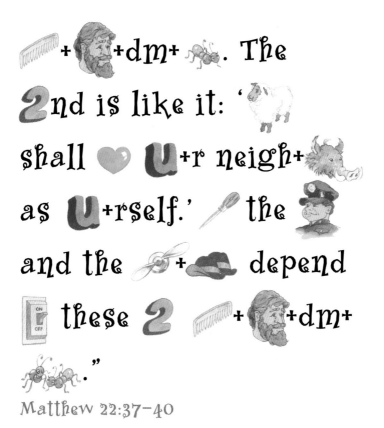

comb + (man's head) +dm+ ant. The **2**nd is like it: ' (sheep) shall ♥ **U**+r neigh+ (boar) as **U**+rself.' (awl) the (policeman) and the (propeller)+ (hat) depend (switch) these **2** comb + (man's head) +dm+ ant. "

Matthew 22:37-40

God Loved the World

Follow the path to eternal life. Along the way you'll find the words to the memory verse. *(Story found on page 98.)*

"For God so loved the world that He gave His only Son, so that every-one who believes in Him will not perish but have eternal life." John 3:16

The Great Commission

Jesus left His followers a big job! Follow the lines from the first balloon to the last to find out what Jesus wants you to do. *(Story found on page 104.)*

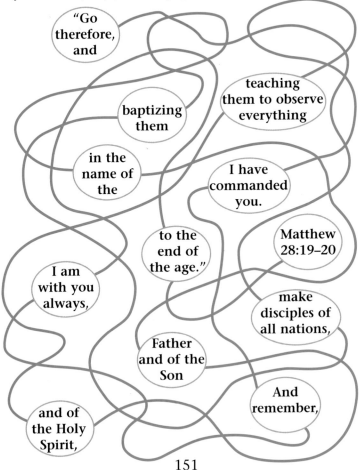

"Go therefore, and

teaching them to observe everything

baptizing them

in the name of the

I have commanded you.

to the end of the age."

Matthew 28:19–20

I am with you always,

make disciples of all nations,

Father and of the Son

And remember,

and of the Holy Spirit,

151

Love

Follow the words of the memory verse through the maze to learn the verse and see what love is. Watch out for wrong words and sidetracks! *(Story found on page 108.)*

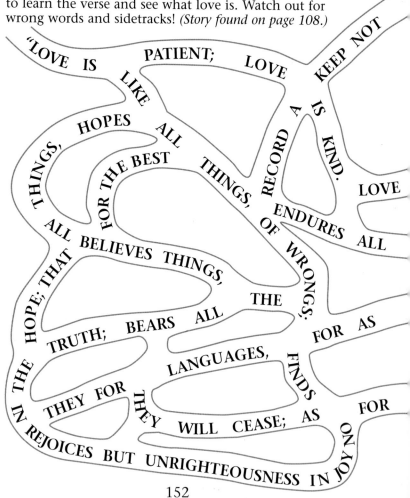

"LOVE IS PATIENT; LOVE IS KIND. KEEP NOT
LIKE RECORD A
HOPES ALL THINGS, LOVE
THINGS, FOR THE BEST ENDURES ALL
ALL BELIEVES THINGS, OF WRONGS;
THE HOPE; THAT THE
TRUTH; BEARS ALL FOR AS
LANGUAGES, FINDS
THEY FOR THEY AS FOR
IN REJOICES BUT UNRIGHTEOUSNESS IN JOY ON WILL CEASE;

152

DOES PROVOKED; ENVY; IS NOT ONLY CONCEITED; DOES NOT BOASTFUL; IS NOT NOT WEIRD. DOES NOT NOT TO FULL IS IMPROPERLY; ACT NOT DOES IS NOT ODD; LOVE SELFISH; THE ONE BUT AS FOR PROPHECIES; THINGS. LOVE NEVER ENDS. ON HAPPEN TOMORROW AS END; IS AN TO COME WILL THEY AND END AN WILL IT WILL COME TO AN END." KNOWLEDGE, IT WILL LOOSE.

1 Corinthians 13:4-8

Fruit of the Spirit

key of Dm

GALATIANS 5:22–23 *(Story found on page 110.)*

154

Once again the verse got mixed up with a picture book and the letters got confused. Say the words for the pictures, replacing some letters. *(Story found on page 118.)*

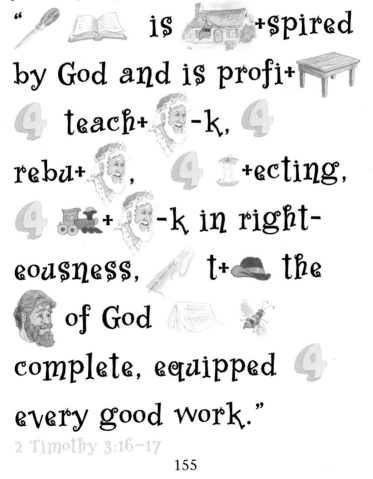

" 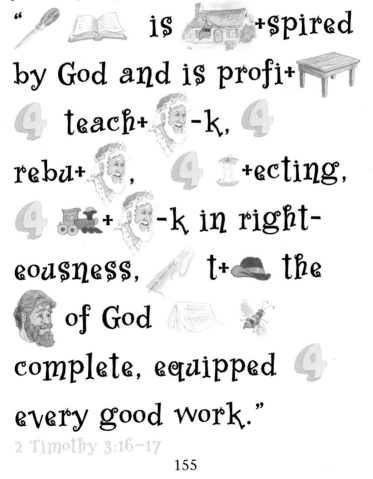 is 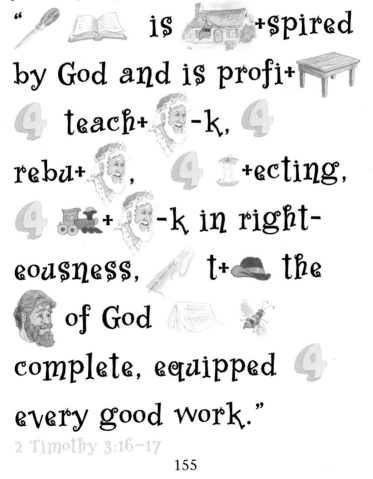 +spired by God and is profi+

4 teach+ -k, 4

rebu+ , 4 +ecting,

4 + -k in right-

eousness, t+ the

 of God

complete, equipped 4

every good work."

2 Timothy 3:16–17

155

Miscellaneous Memorizing Tips

Try these activities. They take a bit more preparation but can be a great aid in helping your children memorize a variety of verses.

Card Search: Write the words of the verse and the reference on 3 x 5 inch cards; then hide them. Have your child search for them—in order if possible. Once found, have your child lay the cards out in order.

Church Memory: Cut two identical church shapes from poster board. Decorate: No. 1 shows the inside with lots of people; No. 2 is the outside with windows and two large doors. Cut along the center and top lines of the doors and fold open. Paste No. 2 on top of No. 1 so that the open doors show the people. Write the verse on the outside or back. (Especially good for verses about the church or gathering together.)

Fill the Hole: On poster board, write the verse with big spaces between words. Around key words, draw and cut out shapes that represent the main thought of the verse (such as crowns, fish, stars, or hearts). Mix up the missing words/shapes and have your child replace them, saying the verse.

Fishers of Verses: Write the words of the verse on fish shapes. Attach paper clips to each. Make a fishing rod out of a straw, string, and a small magnet; then fish for the verse. Each fish is placed on the table in the correct order. (Especially good for "I'll make you fishers of men.")

"Invisible" Verse: Using a white or light-colored wax crayon, print the verse on paper so it's almost invisible. Paint over the whole page with bright watercolors. The verse stands out because no paint sticks to it (as sin can't stick to us when we follow Jesus).

Keepsakes: Make verse keepsakes out of poster board cut as follows:

Bookmark: 1½ by 7 inches

Placemat: 12 by 16 inches

Doorknob hanger: 3 by 8 inches (from the top edge cut in at a slant and make a hole the size of a fifty-cent piece)

Write and illustrate the verse on the keepsake. Laminate.
    Place the bookmark in a favorite book or the child's Bible, the doorknob hanger on the child's bedroom door, and the placemat at the child's place at the table. Each time the child opens the book, enters the room, or eats, he or she can say the verse.

Matching Pairs: Write the verse's words on two sets of cards. Mix them up and turn them upside down. Your child turns over two at a time looking for a pair. Unmatched cards are turned over again. Paired cards are set aside. When all the pairs are found the cards are laid out in order—twice. (Easier game: Use two colors of cards. Harder game: Find pairs in order.)

Memory Hop-Scotch: Draw a hop-scotch shape on the sidewalk or driveway and write a word from the verse in each square. The child throws a stone or nickel into squares, in order, and jumps the hop-scotch. On each throw or jump the child says the square's word and/or the verse to that point.

Nickel Toss or Verse Hop: Write the words of the verse on separate (large) cards. Place the cards randomly on the floor. If playing Nickel Toss, give your child a nickel. Have the child either toss the coin or hop onto the cards—in order. Repeating the verse between tosses or hops reminds the child where to toss/hop next.

Verse Chains: (Good for longer verses.) Cut pieces of paper 1 x 3 inches. Write one word from the verse on each. Make a paper chain: curl the first piece into a circle with the word on the outside, and tape it; curl the second piece *through* the first; and so on. (This represents how we make a chain of believers when we tell others about Jesus—good for witnessing verses.)

Verse Puzzle: Draw a relevant shape (e.g., the stone tablets for the Law, a fish, a crown, a heart) on a large piece of poster board or light cardboard. Write the verse inside the shape. Draw curving puzzle-shaped lines across your verse. Cut out the shape and then cut along the lines. Mix up the pieces. As your child puts the puzzle together, talk about the verse and have the child repeat it.

Word Scramble: (For older children.) Write out the verse, scrambling the letters of some words. Have your child unscramble the letters to find the verse. Rereading the verse each time helps the child memorize it.

L I G H T w a v e
building Christian faith in families

Lightwave Publishing is one of North America's leading developers of quality resources that encourage, assist, and equip parents to build Christian faith in their families. Their products help parents answer their children's questions about the Christian faith, teach them how to make church, Sunday school, and Bible reading more meaningful for their children, provide them with pointers on teaching their children to pray, and much, much more.

Lightwave, together with its various publishing and ministry partners, such as Focus on the Family, has been successfully producing innovative books, music, and games since 1984. Some of their more recent products include *A Parents' Guide to the Spiritual Growth of Children*, *Joy Ride!*, *Mealtime Moments*, and *My Time With God*.

Lightwave also has a fun kids' Web site and an Internet-based newsletter called *Tips and Tools for Spiritual Parenting*. For more information and a complete list of Lightwave products, please visit: **www.lightwavepublishing.com**.